Ambivalence Poetry

All Ranges of Emotions

By
Writer Sky Snow

MAPLE
PUBLISHERS

Ambivalence - Poetry All Ranges of Emotions

Author: Writer Sky Snow

Copyright © Writer Sky Snow (2025)

The right of Writer Sky Snow to be identified as author of this work has been asserted by the author in accordance with section 77 and 78 of the Copyright, Designs and Patents Act 1988.

First Published in 2025

ISBN 978-1-83538-447-3 (Paperback)
      978-1-83538-448-0 (E-Book)

Cover Design and Book Layout by:
    White Magic Studios
    www.whitemagicstudios.co.uk

Published by:
    Maple Publishers
    Fairbourne Drive, Atterbury,
    Milton Keynes,
    MK10 9RG, UK
    www.maplepublishers.com

A CIP catalogue record for this title is available from the British Library.

All rights reserved. No part of this book may be reproduced or translated by any form or by any means, electronic or mechanical, including photocopying, recording or by any information storage and retrieval system without written permission from the author.

The views expressed in this work are solely those of the author and do not necessarily reflect the views of the publisher, and the publisher hereby disclaims any responsibility for them.

This book is dedicated to Joy Russell and Gary Muffet for being my strength in taking care of my daughters; Aurora and Alexis when my health sadly deteriorated.

With this book I honor them wholeheartedly for ensuring my children thrived and remained happy and content.

I will always be grateful, they are much appreciated! When the dark times fell upon me, they were the light that never dare went out.

This book is also dedicated to Alexander Redman for being the hope in the days that were most hopelessly bleak. You always found the best parts of me and brought them to life even when I felt as though I had died. I was lost for a long time but you would always find me and show me that life was a journey to be worth living.

CONTENTS

Chapter one: Corrupted mindset 8
1) Homicidal heart's 9
2) Rose's 10
3) Insomnia mindset 11
4) Ghost of you 12
5) Don't cry 13
6) Better apart 14
7) Hopeful heart 15
8) Independence at its finest 16
9) Trapped marriage 17
10) Little crush 18

Chapter two: Corrupted soul's 19
11) Trauma of the mind 20
12) How I disappear 21
13) Drunk and dramatic 22
14) Momma knows best 23
15) Magical cure 24
16) Unicorns 25
17) Seasonal love 26
18) I don't want me 27
19) Surrounded by thorns 28
20) Find myself 29

Chapter three: Corrupted heart's 30
21) Mockingbird 31
22) Sold her soul 32
23) Comatose 33
24) No 34

25)	Fired	35
26)	Devil's taking over	36
27)	The darkest path	37
28)	A better fame	38
29)	Outgrown	39
30)	Hold on	40

Chapter four: Corrupted hope 41

31)	One, two, three	42
32)	Please Lord	43
33)	House fire	44
34)	The mental health monster	45
35)	Stacey	46
36)	Ring-a-ring-a-roses	47
37)	Bipolar	48
38)	Hunger for word's	49
39)	Circus of dreams	50

Chapter five: Corrupted emotions 51

40)	Lover to find	52
41)	Don't cut	53
42)	When I go	54
43)	Manhood	55
44)	Bunny	56
45)	Recovery	57
46)	Robots	58
47)	Emotional contradiction	59
48)	Remorse	60
49)	Angel's	61
50)	One kiss to fix you	62

Chapter six: Corrupted thoughts 63
51) Sorry 64
52) Ring, ring! 65
53) Love for Momma... 66
54) Lost to prison 67
55) Movie scenes 68
56) Words of corn... 69
57) Slave 70
58) Too late to call 71
59) Actions and fate 72
60) Cardboard box 73

Chapter seven: Corrupted pain 74
61) God's plan.. 75
62) Poorly princess.. 76
63) Run for the hills 77
64) Fur 78
65) Miracle 79
66) Eco home.. 80
67) Safe with you... 81
68) Winters breathing 82
69) Sparkless 83
70) Doves... 84

Chapter eight: Corrupted at best........................... 85
71) Fuck... 86
72) Dead to be breathing....................................... 87
73) You can't see.. 88
74) Dancing with your ghost................................ 89
75) Void 90
76) Furrocious 91

77) Hate him...92
78) Trading lives...93
79) Her mind raced 94
80) Financial democracy 95

Chapter nine: Corrupted senses............................ 96
81) Soldier 97
82) Penny... 98
83) Cancer 99
84) Sober 100
85) Torture the mind.. 101
86) Worse 102
87) Storms 103
88) Devil's and questions 104
89) Frostbite 105
90) Sometimes 106

Chapter ten: Corrupted Ends 107
91) Time 108
92) Runt..109
93) No love 110
94) Let the darkness in...111
95) Bankrupt 112
96) A baby that's Due... 113
97) Pining for you 114
98) Anyone Else..115
99) Eulogy.. 116
100) Ladder To Heaven 117

Chapter one: Corrupted mindset

Homicidal heart's

Another empty bottle,
Another throat you'll throttle,
Tonight, he'll take a life,
Drunk, walking the streets with a bread knife,
So many issues,
No time for those tissues,
Losing all of the euphoria,
Only to sit back and receive nausea,
His heart appears to be broken,
His soul is torn wide open,
He's found himself living in Hell,
Nobody stayed around to wish him well.

Rose's

She knew that she was free,
Still, he wouldn't let her be,
She's always so very stressed,
For life, she did her absolute best,
Mental health, yet she dances away,
For the man she never wanted to marry,
He gave her Rose's, she threw them in the bin,
He gave her cupcakes, she wouldn't take the sin,
He gave her wise words with a verbal curse,
Now she's buying him Rose's in reverse.

Insomnia mindset

Thought's progress into deadly,
No one can speak, it's getting heavy,
Minds fade into hopelessly bleak,
The truth is something that we all seek,
Worlds apart we begin to retreat,
Humbling hearts admit to the defeat,
It's wicked if we just can't sleep,
The pains developed are to keep,
Talking rhymes become bluntly cheap,
Into a pillow, everyone will weep.

Ghost of you

She was holding onto those flowers for hours,
She believed her wife had some superpowers,
They always knew when she was sad,
Every breath hurt when the days are bad,
She cried, "I'm sorry, you really can't save me"
You see she's not visible in reality,
The flowers are now dusty, old and dead,
New crushing pains take over in her head,
Pale, frail, looking just like a ghost,
Something dark that no one can toast,
Hidden words, she dare not to boast,
It's corrupt how sadness became her host.

Don't cry

Darling, don't you cry, they are the loser,
Wipe away the years, you're the amuser,
Your own life, you're the chooser,
They didn't know the diamond that they had,
They couldn't see you when you got sad,
You can move on; it isn't all bad.

Better apart

It wasn't any kind of hypnotic,
However, it was truly symbolic,
They couldn't handle it,
So, they dismantled it,
It died very strongly,
They agreed so wrongly,
They're glad you're gone,
They're never happy for too long,
Let them go, let them go,
Allow them to awake and rise,
Let them free to go,
To a compelling sunrise.

Hopeful heart

My heart, it always breaks,
My time, she always takes,
My world is at its gruesome end,
My love is now only pretend,
My mind is forever open,
My thoughts will always be hoping.

Independence at its finest

He was the first one to leave,
She was the last one to grieve,
If only he could of knew,
How much she did for you,
He took her mind when he left,
Losing her heart, it was theft,
She didn't know that she'd be okay,
Gracefully independent within a day.

Trapped marriage

Will you marry me?
And our baby, will you carry for me?
Will you move right in with me?
Why's the dinner never cooked?
Why's our bedroom never shooked,
Why didn't you like the emerald ring?
Was I just not your kind of thing?
Can you give me your heart?
Can I collect everything from the start?
Put your whole world into my hands!
Without me, don't you dare to make any plans!
I can feel it deep within my soul,
They've got my mind and I've lost control,
I didn't want to agree to anything,
Trying to marry me with your ex's ring,
You want me to hold your baby,
You've already given it to another lady,
You want me to marry you,
But I just don't care like you do.

Little crush

Hold back the river, it isn't sunset yet,
I know your Mommy didn't like me much,
This time I was easier to forget,
My mistake, my stupid little crush,
I'm hurting on the inside,
They're ready to swallow their pride,
Time stood still when it could've flied,
Admittedly neither of us ever tried.

Chapter two: Corrupted soul's

Trauma of the mind

Please don't leave me alone,
Within you, I've now found my home,
I cannot survive without your warmth,
Festering thoughts in my mind will swarmth,
Every second I'm getting closer to death,
Losing my sanity, I've lost all control,
Something blue like crushed crystal mesh,
Lavished like a laced living doll,
I was his only unforgettable regret,
To not normalize all of the neglect,
Another heartbreak, another sudden reject,
I'm the type of trauma that's better to forget.

How I disappear

I won't fall in love again,
Just to break, break, break,
The way I did back then,
For you to take, take, take,
I could see the evil lurking within,
I would fall far from any grace,
Bruises buried beneath the skin,
Lost to the devil, left with no trace.

Drunk and dramatic

He was drinking whiskey,
Letting her get frisky,
Taking pictures, snap, snap,
Hoping that he could win her back,
He couldn't put the bottle down,
Violent rambles throughout the town,
He's only happy when he's wasted,
Alcohol is the only happiness he's tasted.

Momma knows best

Oh' honey, it's just not that funny,
You let the winter in and refused all sunny,
I just can't reach out to your wicked ways,
I'll leave you in just a number of days,
As beauty fades you are irrevocably replaced,
Anything to be with a skinnier, thinner waist,
I've always thought that the world was obese,
It lacks personality, a generational tease,
Beat to heart, beat to the chest,
Funny how 'Mother's' always know what's best,
There's no settling until she's put to rest,
Our Momma tried to teach us about life's test.

Magical cure

Hello? I think I need a genie,
I need the magic to cure,
Life can be such a meanie,
For all the trivials we endure,
Where did the rainbows go?
Where has the sky gone?
My world around me will snow,
Until I can fix what is wrong.

Unicorns

A unicorn walks,
A glittery sky talks,
Of beauty and wisdom,
In all of nature's kingdom,
Gracious gentle leafs,
Restore all of our beliefs,
Magical smells appear,
Another unicorn is near.

Seasonal love

Wishes and kisses from a blue butterfly,

It's the only way to make a flower feel high,

Love from a season that's ended so strong,

Perhaps a butterfly and a flower isn't so wrong,

Yet death surrounds a pianos tune,

Flowers are graceful to bracefully bloom,

It's peaceful on the other side you must see,

But this flower didn't turn out to what it could be.

I don't want me

Oh my god, it hurts, it's the worst,

You didn't want me and now I don't want me,

I couldn't replace the frown upon your face,

Did you ever want me? Or were the words forged?

A knife into my brain, a bullet into my heart,

You used to love me, the world would fly above me,

Now every word is a curse and a sword is drawn,

I want to leave but my mind has unraveled itself.

Surrounded by thorns

Every flower has it's dainty thorn,
She wished she was never born,
She was silent, her world was torn,
For another friend, she could not mourn,
She found peace in a simple acorn,
But her lies began to swirl and scorn,
In life, she's just another forgotten pawn,
Is the grass greener on the other lawn?
She's not safe, she's not humble,
Her words unsavaged to be nimble,
Watching her shadow into the moonlight,
For once she can feel the magic within seight.

Find myself

Time can't heal, time just won't heal,
All the demons inside my head that I can feel,
I find it hard to know what is actually real,
Nobody understands or feels my ordeal,
We just wait to hang around,
For the day when our feet are off the ground,
Everybody wants to be safe and sound,
All of us are lost and we wish to be found.

Chapter three: Corrupted heart's

Mockingbird

He didn't understand when she'd hit him,
He was innocent with barely any sin,
Her anger would only just begin,
Her words, you can hear she wants to win,
She cheated too, walls were frail and thin,
Treating him as a pauper and not as a king,
She was the angel without a feather or wing,
He's pushed down the stairs, it's time for the Mockingbird to sing.

Sold her soul

She couldn't understand any of life's level,
She sold her soul to the conjuring devil,
She yearned for the fame and all of the glory,
Soulless, she's lost within her own story,
In all of the thoughts and all of the pain,
She going completely and utterly insane,
All the memories she just cannot tame,
Only the suffering and agony will remain.

Comatose

She was there when you was all alone,

She's the one to still offer you a home,

She calls and you ignored the phone,

The next call you won't like, dial tone,

"Hello, I'm a doctor and your mother's quite sick,

I don't want to worry you but you'll have to be quick"

You run to your Momma, begging to heal all,

That's when into a coma she will silently fall,

Without your Momma, you don't stand so tall,

If only you'd have answered when she bothered to call.

No

She's loved,
She's lost,
She's gained,
She moved on,
She let go,
They came back,
She laughed,
Shaking her head 'no'.

Fired

Rose's are red but he's so tired,
Skies are blue but he's just been fired,
He feels such a failure at best,
Always the last one to get the test,
It was his mistake you must know,
He let hope for a promotion go,
Under all of the stress he had lost his glory,
He knows he's at the start of this story.

Devil's taking over

The devil lurks within your brain,

The devil's taken over, you are now insane,

He doesn't share you, do you feel the same?

He's hiding beneath you, he just will not tame,

Whom are you? Do you remember your own name?

You're the devil now, there is no chance for fame,

All thoughts become an overfilled ashtray,

The light you can no longer stumble to find,

You cannot steer away from the devil's pathway,

Weak to the bones and cold in the mind.

The darkest path

All the potions, notions and emotions cannot heal me,

Walking through town alone, I feel such a freak,

On the darkest path there ever could be,

Lost my voice, I can no longer speak,

The sins are darker now, it is fierce,

I'm lost to the darkness just as I had feared,

My body was a punch bag to be pierced,

My pain wouldn't let go, my thoughts uncleared.

A better fame

I've got no money for the poor,
I've lost all digits in my bank account,
I can't donate my money anymore,
I need to work for any amount,
I'm grounded, I cannot afford to live,
No luxuries are to my name,
I'm lost because I cannot give,
A road to a better fame.

Outgrown

Dear Dad, it would mean a lot to me,

For you to see the adult I've turned out to be,

I always did my best for you to be proud,

Until the day you told me to never come around,

Dear Dad, it's been years since I saw your face,

I hoped you'd come back, that you'd found your place,

Years passed by and I would soon know,

I was the child that you'd outgrow.

Hold on

With you, I hold out all of the faith,
That I'm not just some human waste,
I await my purpose to truly succumb,
If I told you the truth, would you run?
Hold on, be strong, it doesn't last,
Tick-Tock the chimes fly by so fast,
Breathe deep, let it all rest to peace,
Or your sadness will never cease.

Ambivalence – Poetry All Ranges of Emotions

Chapter four: Corrupted hope

One, two, three...

One, two, three, I think this one is for me,

Four, five, six, she's playing games and tricks,

Seven, eight, nine, she's left me feeling not so fine,

Ten, eleven, twelve, she knocked me off the shelf,

Thirteen, fourteen, fifteen, on me she simply isn't keen.

Please Lord

Please Lord, show me the way,

Please Lord, let me be if I may,

Please Lord, my pain is here today,

Please Lord, look after my children as I fade away,

Please Lord, give me the strength to stay,

Please Lord, hold me as I begin to sway.

House fire

There was no time, only thick grey smoke,

A family of five in the house begin to choke,

There were no windows that'd open to escape,

The morning came and it was far too late,

The house was turned into a crumbled statue,

Fear of the house would always latch to you,

At night I wondered what had happened to their soul,

I couldn't see them, the fire took complete control.

The mental health monster

I'm terrified that he'll see my harrowing eyes,
That's where the monster likes to hide,
I'm not myself, I'm not a human anymore,
I wear glasses to hide but now I'm sore,
My health is down, I'm not so tough,
He now sees me as a diamond in the rough,
Inside my brain I begin to suffocate,
I know one day he'll leave and it'll be too late.

Stacey

Shadows surround the empty hallway,
Just get away Stacey, get away,
It's a horror show, you shouldn't stay,
Come on Stacey, get through the day,
I only wished for you to be okay,
Stacey had to have it her way,
Stubbing cigarettes out into an ashtray,
Stacey, please if I may,
High on a beach, Stacey will lay.

Ring-a-ring-a-roses

Ring-a-ring-a-roses we all must be dead,
The kid's have got a gun to eachothers head,
Once babies, now teenagers getting out of bed,
Ring-a-ring-a-roses we all must be gone,
Kid's hating one another, it's all so wrong,
Once a lullaby, now a heavy drum and bass song.

Bipolar

The doctor's said she would never get better,
From here on it's only stormy weather,
To fall in love, for her it's a never,
A bipolar mess, eyes that are always wetter,
A roller-coaster that would soon untether.

Hunger for word's

Words are a curse and that's not the worst,

There's a rumble in my tummy for another verse,

And if for a second I cannot write my mind,

I'd have to take back every autograph I'd signed,

What if Mom cannot save me?

What if Dad really does hate me?

These thoughts would move me,

To the tomb too be.

Circus of dreams

Hold onto your merry-go-round,
It's trinkets never really made a sound,
I just wanted you all to be so proud,
Always profound to be extra and loud,
Sweet dreams were made for you,
Nightmares fade away as they do,
All for your soft soulful smile,
I'll be having good dreams for a while.

Chapter five: Corrupted emotions

Lover to find

There's a tickle in my throat,
I've always been the one to gloat,
Stranded alone in my paddling boat,
For society, I forgot how to float,
We all want peace and serenity,
Trying to balance out our tranquility,
Searching for a life of stability,
Hoping that my lover will find me.

Don't cut

Please don't cut, please don't cut,
Give me your hand, I'll help you out of this rut,
I hate to see that your hurting yourself,
Losing your mind into a spiral of mental health,
How I wish that I could take your pain away,
But in a critical loop you seem to say.

When I go

When I go, lay me down,
When I go, remember me as a class clown,
When I go, remove my thorny crown,
When I go, I'll finally be free,
When I go, don't hold it against me,
When I go, it's everyone's destiny.

Manhood

The echoes of his heartbeat,
Would bring all of the girls to their feet,
Nobody could see through his deceit,
A lover, he could never choose,
He always thought it'd be too much to confuse,
His manhood, he feared to lose.

Bunny

A rabbit ran down the hill,
Ears pinned back for the thrill,
The truth is hard to swallow like a pill,
At the bottom, the rabbit ran still,
Jumping drastically to avoid the kill.

Recovery

I don't think I'd survive another surgery,
I've spent my life in a doctor's severity,
Moving from one hospital bed to another,
I've still not had the time to recover,
All of my life I've been in hospital sick,
Praying for a cure to heal me quick.

Robots

Robots have more feeling than she,
Robots have it better, a technicality,
Robots don't need human eyes to see,
Robots can live knowing they're never free,
Robots don't feel emotions drastically,
Robots survive without needing any glee.

Emotional contradiction

I remember when we first kissed,
It was something that I've missed,
Now I'm something you've dismissed,
I was soon to be tricked,
I was never the one to be picked,
I'm brave when my emotions contradict.

Remorse

The simple things in life that kept her sane,
Has left her at worlds end and she's all alone,
Her wickedness she could not tame,
Always moving from a home to another home,
She wasn't wanted by any of the fools,
She'd rather keep herself with caution,
Than be with any of these tools,
This was the time she'd gather remorsion.

Angel's

I hold my angel close to my heart,
To hug me whilst I fall apart,
My Angel's wings wrap around me,
To prepare me for the world to be,
I thought I was on this path alone,
My angel is with me, inside my cozy home,
Warm and safe I'll sleep at night,
A kiss on the forehead and it's goodnight.

One kiss to fix you

As cold and heartless as you once were,
Others feelings, you'd help yourself and stir,
Nothing but another failed reject,
There was nothing close for you to protect,
I can see all of your venomous pain,
I can see your eyes full of rain,
If only I could learn to kiss you better,
It tares me up inside that your eyes get wetter.

Chapter six: Corrupted thoughts

Sorry

In her head, in her mind she's so sorry,
She didn't want anybody to worry,
She knew everyone in life had a secret,
No one was able to be quiet and keep it,
She's sorry that she cannot forgive,
She's sorry that you're on your own,
In this world she cannot be strong to live,
Without a heart, nowhere is a home.

Ring, ring!

Ring, ring, there's a bell inside her head,
A voice comes to life and wishes her dead,
The tears keep running, she doesn't know why,
Tears fall from her face, she will always cry,
Ring, ring, there's a voice inside of her mind,
There is a pain inside that she wishes to rewind,
She wanted him back, yet he'd only sigh,
Because of him, her tears will never run dry.

Love for Momma

My Momma always told me,
One day someone will hold onto me,
My Momma always gave me,
The best advice in life to save me,
I'd do anything for my Momma,
She helped me escape all of life's drama,
And now I don't feel like a lost llama,
I think my Momma introduced some to karma.

Lost to prison

He's lost himself again,
He is not like other gentlemen,
He tried but he can't get back up,
For him, all of the doors are shut,
He can't watch the news, it makes him sad,
He can't watch the news, it makes him feel bad,
He remembered killing was the best time he'd had,
He's on the news, he is in prison, you'll be glad.

Movie scenes

Breaking down, walls of entry,
Tearing the world into smithereens,
Heart's would tremble aplenty,
For the false love in movie scenes,
Teeth crumbling for the life of a smile,
Eyes glistening for the sights of freedom,
I wish that I could stay for a while,
But your world isn't my kingdom.

Words of corn

His talk is cheap, his words were corn,
He wished that he was never born,
Through his heartache he was torn,
He told his wife he'd still smile, he'd sworn,
He lost his wife, he will always mourn.

Slave

I love it when you say goodbye,
I love it when you make up another lie,
I'm nowhere near within your sights,
That's when I leave, my body still fights,
There's a hole inside of my heart,
I think you put it there from the very start,
To love is to be blissfully brave,
Loving the wrong one will leave you a slave.

Too late to call

Her face is wearing to pale and thin,
Into a battle that she cannot win,
She's violently placed into societies bin,
Her thoughts are her only sin,
Negative thoughts would quickly begin,
A phone call awaits for her next of kin.

Actions and fate

They broke up, did you not hear?
They said they've shed their final tear,
Together yet alone for under a year,
They'll lose eachother just as they'd fear,
Do you know how loud actions are when they speak?
Bringing drowning tears to the sightly weak,
All of the words, they are proof to the defeat,
For the final time, they fall to their feet.

Cardboard box

Living in a cardboard box,
It's better than living on these rocks,
No materials, no shoes or socks,
Living free like a mighty red fox,
It's another cloudy day,
Pushing the positive thoughts away,
Another storm is stumbling ahead,
Another bottle just to be fed.

God's plan

She had a diamond in her eye,
A bay window, at night she'd lye,
She knew how her life was a big mess,
Her pain, nobody could try to guess,
In the ground she yearned to rest,
God had a plan, she was one of the best.

Poorly princess

We met in a run down ghostly pub,
She was poorly using vapor rub,
The flu had made her feel so rough,
But beauty inside was always enough,
Soft to the touch, her skin like cotton,
She smiled through a flu so rotten,
I was the man she had forgotten,
To fall for her would be a constant.

Run for the hills

It's so very sick for us to reminisce,
How awful it was to have our first kiss,
It's something that nobody can miss,
With you there was never any trust,
Because of you there wasn't an us,
To run away from you is a must.

Fur

As sunny as it was, as bright as it were,
She caught him wearing real fox fur,
Disgusted by the likes of him,
How he'd love to lay in animal skin,
She had to leave, to run far away,
She prays for the animals lost each day.

Miracle

It's morning, did you sleep well?
Did you dream of love or just Hell?
The sun is rising eagerly fast,
Filling the hours in the hour glass,
Warm and welcome to a fresh new day,
Always checking the bank for a payday,
Breakfast time, enjoy some cereal,
Every day is a brand new miracle.

Eco home

He used to be emo,
Now he is kind of eco,
Emotions were his all time disaster,
Time kept going by faster and faster,
He found peace in living on his own,
Warm and cozy in his eco home.

Safe with you

I just know that you love me,
Right here is where I want to be,
Warm within your peaceful presence,
I'm no longer surviving on the defense,
I know that I love you more though,
You've saved me in ways you'd never know.

Winters breathing

Greasy hair, pale skin, winter is breathing,
Dry eyes, cracked lips, ready for dying,
Poison willfully flowing through the body,
Ice cold, the streets are freezing,
Icicles onto a hat, it's now styling,
This time of year is always shoddy,
Season of uneasing, wheezing and sneezing,
Frozen onto the town's rock hard bench,
A needle hanging out from an arm,
Yet the smile of joy is still present,
Another body to the potent stench,
The whole world, yet so much harm,
There are prayers the Angel's should've sent.

Sparkless

She's lost the sparkle in her eyes,
She's in a state, she always cries,
A river of tears for what they once had,
No longer together through the good and bad,
Unbreak her heart, give her another chance,
Love and loyalty is now just a trance,
She's losing faith without him by her side,
A lump in the throat, a sudden swallow of pride,
He will never follow her again,
She won't ever forget how it was back then,
Her eyes are dull from the crying for days,
How to move on? She questions in a haze.

Doves

Sweet bells are ringing,
Doves are gathered singing,
Living for those tender dreams,
Now we know life is not what it seems,
And there she goes again,
She's taken absolutely everything,
I know she is gone when,
The Doves no longer sing.

Chapter eight: Corrupted at best

Fuck

I'm losing my faith, I'm losing my mind,
All to be kept silenced and stupidly kind,
What the fuck is life all about?
Everyone is deaf, no one can hear me shout,
Fuck you, fuck this, fuck all of that,
Fuck trying to be a princess to an unloyal twat,
Desperate on your knees, are you joking me?
Saying that your sorry yet again for hitting me,

Fuck you, fuck this, fuck all of that,
You're just a violent thug, a typical prat,
Even when you'd be sober you'd fly off the handle,
Smashed my head against the mantle to be the next scandal,
I was never getting out of this alive anyway,
Although I could never die the merry way,
Fuck it all, I escaped, to only leave my mind behind,
Lost my mind, bind to be blind, if only our stars had never aligned.

Dead to be breathing

Get the hell away from me,
I just know that your never sorry,
Get the fuck off of my skin,
Spiders inside my eyes are crawling within,
A devil's tongue is ready to pursue,
With no thoughts to be thought through,

Just a zombie of a mother, dead to be breathing,
No hope left for the alive to be leaving,
Once bitten, now three times the fury,
Convicted guilty without a judge or jury,
Now she's gathered her reminiscent death,
He made sure that she had nothing left.

You can't see

Mental health sucks, you can barely see that it is there,

A thread of luck and they have lost some hair,

Stress induced, medications fed until you are full,

It mongs you out leaving eyes of dull, societies mule,

What do you see? It's not me, It's not me,

Locked inside a cage within my own head,

Personalities torn into a complex trauma diagnosis,

Every one of us is screaming but we are so damn hopeless,

We're all crying in the same hollow body,

Begging for anyone to really try to love me,

You can't see mental health, but it is there,

It's a diagnosis that I am ashamed to wear.

Dancing with your ghost

I won't sleep for days just so that I can see your ghost,
You will always be the one that I've loved and missed the most,
With your ghost, I'm dancing as if you never went away,
Closer than most, closer than those that nimble pray,
I can only see you if I do not sleep or eventually rest,
I'll dance with you, of all the time it's now that is the best,

I know that if I don't sleep, I'll be moved onto your side,
We can both be ghosts forever, dancing ghosts don't hide,
I'm getting blindly tired, I fell into an unwanted sleep,
I awoke to learn that your ghost isn't mine to keep,
I've had no sleep for four night's and four day's,
To dance with your ghost in the moonlights magical rays.

Void

Hold on, be careful what you wish for,
You've stolen more candy from the forbidden drawer,
It's crushed and crumbled into the camouflage floor,
You took my tainted soul from It's very core,

That's when I realized I should have stayed at home,
Comparing chocolates to a genuine golden honey comb,
Within my freedom, it's my choice where I shall roam,
Suddenly I'm fractured like our gormless garden gnome,

In life it was easier for us all to choose to avoid,
Destroyed in the sentiments that we once heartedly enjoyed,
Unaware, we are all trapped in the noiseless void,
Stepping on eggshells, wondering why is everyone annoyed?

Furrocious

I can taste the explosions of his tortured emotions,
Going through the notions that are erosions of the oceans,
Devotions just to hope that the mind and heart opens,
Taking tokens for the potions and motions of the lotions,
No matter the outcome, we are all far too emotional,
Giving up our free time like it is somehow negotiable,
Appearing unsociable to try and become a kind of devotional,
A cheesy fake smile so that we can one day look approachable,
Hit like hail stones, we are appearing freakishly emotionless,
Choosing between the boastfullness and the homelessness,
There is no wholesomeness in being fully hopelessness,
Even the most soulfullness can feel the burn of the feriousness.

Hate him

I hate him, I wish him the absolute worst,

I hope he leaves her and I hope his heart will burst,

I hope all the love is dispersed and quickly reversed,

I hope every wish in the wishing well is immersed and cursed,

I hope that he gets so sick that he cannot be nursed,

I hope all of his payments will never be reimbursed,

I hope every thought he has about himself is coerced,

I hope no matter how much water he drinks, he still feels the thirst,

I hate him, it was easier to let him go first,

Instead of remaining stuck and being fully immersed,

I hope he lives on the lies of the distrust,

I hope he forgets me just as we had rehearsed.

Trading lives

Damn it! I loved her but she gave me the ultimate shade,
I was a heart that was soon afraid to be played,
She was in my grade but her IQ was delayed,
She was quick to persuade anyone to put down the blade,
You see she was betrayed of the abuse her parent's displayed,

Her house was constantly surveyed for all kinds of a raid,
Against the parents and the police, she never obeyed,
I noticed her emotions were long to be decayed,
She used to hide on the pier and in the arcade,

Years and years, she had suffered the same charade,
She prayed, hoping that she would be unmade,
Quickly the police force themselves in to evade,
To save her Mother, her own life she would trade.

Her mind raced

She danced in the Hawaiian clubs and came up to me,
She held my hands as if it was so easily,
Her eyes raced and paced somehow stone cold but sneakily,
Like she didn't want me to know she was greedily gleefully,

She told me of how she would dream so peacefully,
Up until the heartbreak she had to endure recently,
Her parents were controlling and never leniently,
She just wanted a frequency of decency,

Her mind raced from slow to ultra speedily,
Her parents came to the club and smiled evilly,
They shrugged their shoulders for she was dreamfully,
They shaved her head for she had been deceitfully.

Financial democracy

Classic, the heart is fundamentally fractured,
Dedications at a loss to the needy ones of manufactured,
Just a silhouettes shadow that is ready to be captured,
Losing everyone into the solar system to be enraptured,

It's disgusting that it is upon maternal instinct,
Hands fall away when they were once linked,
As quick as a firefly that is fast to be blinked,
Ignoring the truth that appears distinct,

A sudden rush to the bones of extra unwanted hormones,
Every mother is fed off to their own war zones,
A baby can scream and cry in four tones,
Unappreciated and alone, the mothers hold out hope for loans.

Chapter nine: Corrupted senses

Soldier

Cradle the hunger, it's for the fierce to enjoy,
Society is set out angry and ready to destroy,
No more jobs are left to ever employ,
Sadness to the step, never to experience any joy,

Hands wash away the sins into the river,
Leaving the soul to shiver and quiver,
Gold is sold and sadly so is silver,
There's evil in a smile that won't calm to deliver,

In the the little finger there is utter class,
To the eyes that cry and turn to glass,
More added heartache that will never pass,
All that is left is a soldier and some brass.

Penny

Color me in an tell me that I am terrific,
Don't go over the lines as I'm not a statistic,
Give me all of the colors, make me blend into horrific,
Call me magic, magnificent and majestic,

Leave the rainbows alone, they don't want to be here,
Take my freedom, I am still the same shade,
Lay the roses down whilst my Mother wipes away a tear,
Because it really mattered what color my skin was to meet the blade,

Go on, spit raps, split knee caps for the difference is I,
Salivate the venom into the wounds of many,
Take my eyeballs out of my head to batter and fry,
Make me bleed, beg for my life whilst I spit a pretty penny.

Cancer

I can't handle it, this pain wasn't meant to be mine,
But you still passed it on to me thinking that it's fine,
I was out here drawing chalk but you crossed the line,
Now I'm laying here numb with a scratch into my spine,

I can barely walk yet you can still get up and run,
I've been left all alone whilst your having all of the fun,
I'm facing the harshest winter, whilst your soaking up the sun,
I'm fighting a losing battle that you have already won,

These games keep me in circles and you are to blame,
You keep on changing up on us, yet I remain the same,
I've been left alone and my thoughts are far from tame,
I was the crumpled picture but you are just the frame.

Sober

Echoes in the walls are proving to hold their silence,
Pretending that we do not know when we hear the sirens,
The people begged, prayed and would begin to sing,
Desperately looking for a sign of faith in anything,

Looking in the mirror, oh' dear I'm the bad guy,
Sirens get louder and the neighbors do cry,
Broken glass in a fist fight whilst riding shotgun,
Peeling back the latex of a hot loaded gun,

There's no turning back with the crimes that we attract,
Born to lie, born to ignore every single fact,
Just one single shot, bang! It's all finally over,
If only one member of this family could've gotten sober.

Torture the mind

Emotions are ignored and placed into societies blender,

Just the dark, forgotten, the ultimate defender,

A life of hate that is too far from splendor,

Hit rock bottom, facing the world that is not so tender,

The pretender, they're offended by the sincerity of torture,

Yelling at the top of our lungs in hope of a departure,

A simple butcher with a knife that is claimed to nurture,

Abandoned in the middle of the deserts, it's a right scorcher,

Shirts are blood stained whilst the innocents are caned,

Nothing to ever give and nothing to never be gained,

Handcuffed to the system of demise, they are chained,

More hurting for the hearts that cannot be explained.

Worse

Come on take it, fake it until you make it,

Grit your pearly teeth like you've never hated it,

Cover up your eyes and switch those elephant ears off,

You are only secondhand clothes and I'm the hungry moth,

Twist your own arm, cry when nobody is around,

Write your goodbye letters, get ready to meet the Hell hound,

Burn the life that you had before, sit back the warming flames,

Run a marathon in wonder that in time your heart tames,

Drink the life in the cup that you are served,

Don't you dare tell anybody that your life isn't what you deserved,

Live with the memories, tragedies of the bluntforced curse,

Don't lie to yourself that your own life has present worse.

Storms

There's an odd calm before the dreaded storm,
Too many souls have wished they were not born,
Diamonds fall into the dirt of the Earth,
Too many souls in this world have forgotten their worth,

Shadows in the night that will mask your face,
Pulling at your fake lashes to put you in to place,
Glassy doe eyes with a common reset filter,
More darkness in the mind it could have killed her,

Reset the patience to be hospital inducing bound,
Frozen to the spot, you cannot turn around,
Look around, every single person has a perpetual past,
It is always up to us if we let the storms last.

Devil's and questions

Get away from me, all that I'm left with is Devil's and questions,

Bleeding from the heart, I'm hoping for any kind of healing suggestions,

I hate you, I breathe in your lies and I still need to burn this tattoo,

You look away every part of me and everything that I knew,

My skin crawls like a slithering snake,

Whenever I hear them say your name,

Frostbite

His hands are nimble, his mind races to a crowded place,

Drugs into his system, he cannot feel his face,

He has been missing and he has left no trace,

He is dancing away with the fairies so he can feel the embrace,

Her hands are cold and frozen to the frostbite,

She is desperately searching for him with a bright light,

Stumbling onto sticks and stones, climbing mountains of any height,

She reassures herself that life is alright whilst she wonders into the night,

They could never find each other, it is really quite sad,

She remembered everything of the life that they had,

He wrote his last words onto a torn up notepad,

By the time that she found it, she realized she had lost her Dad.

Sometimes

It's like I scream so loud but no one can hear me,

Sometimes I want to laugh, sometimes I want to cry,

Trapped in rusty shackles, I beg to only be free,

Sometimes I love to live life, sometimes I wish to die,

Sometimes I want to hide, sometimes I want to be found,

They can't hear me but I swear I'm screaming out so loud,

Sometimes like a balloon I fly to the sky, sometimes I crash to the ground,

I appear as a facade of disappointment wanting anyone to be proud,

I'm screaming for the world to notice my feelings,

Sometimes I wish that you loved me like you loved getting high,

I'm screaming the roof off of places, there is no ceilings,

Sometimes I wish and wonder if the rivers will run dry.

Chapter ten: Corrupted Ends

Time

Time is to have patience, time is to stay calm with grace,

Time is to withhold the pains upon your gorgeous face,

Time ticks away faster than anyone can jumpedly run,

Time is spaces between the moon and the sun,

Time is to let it hurt you until it cannot hurt you anymore,

Time is to love and miss somebody until your heart is sore,

Time is to cleverly separate the bliss from all of the gore,

Time is to wonderingly wait for what it has in store,

Time is to hold onto a lucky placed juvenile wonder,

Time is to embrace any weather and separate the thunder,

Time is to humbly accept the pressures that you're under,

Time is to understand that we are humanities blunder.

Runt

Stop that, how dare you talk back like that,
Silly wannabe Santa with no original hat,
Crooked teeth with a hideous thigh gap,
Too many keys on this keyboard to tap,
Breaking faith for a bottle of spiced gin,
Festering thoughts swirl to let a demon in,

Rosy cheeks with the crunch of a candy cane,
Blue eyes to make the saneness insane,
Boots that have been worn right through to the sole,
And empty shell, empty skeleton with no soul,
Brave like the weak, needy and brunt,
Deep of the litter yet proven to be the runt.

No love

It all started when I lost my mother,
It all started when I had no love from a lover,
Another pillow over the face to set in and smother,
Echoes of silence, not even I could love her,

Vape and tape that mouth crystal clear shut,
Ignoring every sense and everything you feel on your gutt,
Moaning the what if and the questionable but,
Dig yourself the grave, only you can climb out of this rut,

I'm getting pretty sick of the words I cannot write,
I can't forgive the pain that lives inside my heart,
I'm too tired to carry on and continue to fight,
I lost my mother, no love from a lover, that was the start.

Let the darkness in

How can you touch me when I am not yours,

How can you hate me when I don't know you of course,

What was that taste of vinegar you'd left in my mouth,

Like a copper coin that ended up down south,

This isn't right and I know that you know,

Your the darkness of the depths that I dare not to go,

Every stick and stone to take my home,

Trapped like 'The Simpsons' in a giant glass dome,

Get away from me, leave me to my peace and tranquility,

Leave me alone or I'll promise you'll know what it's like to be a fatality,

Get out of my house, you are not welcome here,

To let the darkness in, is my biggest fear.

Bankrupt

The black roses are hung, it is a catastrophe,
It's a genuine picture perfect fantasy,
To meet the reaper, he appeared happily,
Into the darkness I walk gallantly,
I would crawl and duck to meet her majesty,
But her death was a world wide tragedy,
Somewhere far into the purple like galaxy,
The innocent shall smile bashfully,
We had hope in our hearts anxiously,
The world sits back to look lazily,
Hate in our hearts disappear callously,
Just to endure another tragedy,
Searching for a hero in the west valiantly,
Feeling and enduring every emotion damnably,
This road is too long and we're in agony,
We need a new hope and a new strategy,
Humming the songs of bohemian rhapsody,
Our smiles hide the country of our bankruptcy.

A baby that's Due

I look for you in a world of destruction,
Every child faces a kind of abduction,
I left my job before my induction,
Deluded minds fathoming a new construction,
We burned into flames for the production,
Hoping that the shops shelves offers a reduction,
We hover around everyone's vibes, magnetic,
Dreaming of a life that is aesthetic,
Even the words of the euphoria and poetic,
Crumble into a sentence that is synthetic,
Claiming our energies will remain kinetic,
We wake in the mornings, feeling that we're energetic,
Walking down the same roads, I will wait,
To hold you again so that I'll feel great,
Absorbing the love and disowning the hate,
These walls can talk but I can see straight,
You are the wheels whenever I rollerskate,
I will wait for you until the due date.

Pining for you

Stop your whining,
She is not worth the mining,
Anyone else you could be dining,
The stars for you never stopped shining,
You are everything, you are defining,

Give it a chance, good things are aligning,
Let the devil's work start declining,
Gather your loved ones, they are combining,
There is love, even in the underlining,
Just like a posh chair, you are reclining,
Into a life where there is no pining.

Anyone Else

Out into the cold and rubbed into the dirt,
An angry blunder as the words do blurt,
Anyone he'd dance with and jokingly flirt,
Anyone that has the shorter mini skirt,
Feeling utterly alone at a packed concert,
Never here for the main course, just desert,

Tear stained face, blood stained shirt,
Dripping down the chin is vanilla yoghurt,
More drama than patience there is to insert,
It will all be proven to be a controvert,
More pain in the chest just to really hurt,
A ton of added pain to really make the mind spurt.

Eulogy

I'm drunk and giving the eulogy,
It's dark, get these people away from me,
I must have fallen out of the family tree,
I look for them but they cannot see,
I am just I, there is no we,
Put that into slow motion,
Downgrade every single emotion,
Take away my wholesome devotion,
Riding with the waves, facing every notion,
Accidentally drinking Alice's small potion,
I'm tired of the silence, tired of the tears,
Alone and abandoned for too many years,
They look down on me, my once loved peers,
I'll crash my car using multiple gears,
I'll weaponise the trauma to reduce all of my fears.

Ladder To Heaven

On a starry night, I question where are you?
I crumble to ask why you didn't take me too,
A sky of purple, what have you done with the blue?
I'd climb the ladder to heaven but I grew,
Why did you leave me here? Where did you go?
Now everyday for me without you is just winter snow,
I've misplaced my light, I've lost my glow,
Alone in this boat I must row,
I know it was your time, but I'm not okay with that,
I mimic your voice in my offensive chav hat,
Upon the stars, alone I am sat,
I want you back like the nights need a bat,
One day when it's right to be together again,
I'll hold you into my arms to be your top ten,
I'd feel at peace, at my all time zen,
I'd love you as I always did back when.